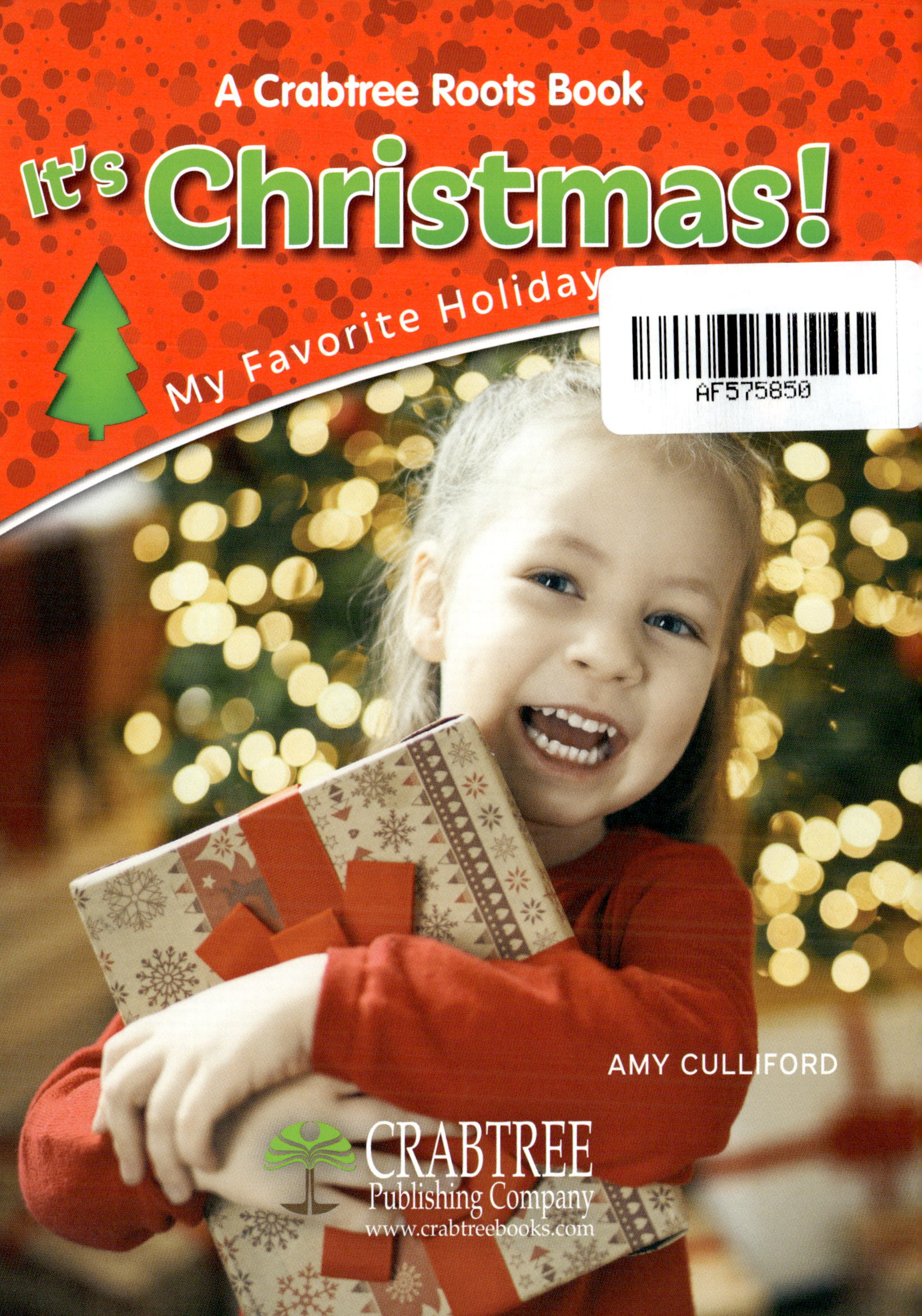
A Crabtree Roots Book
It's Christmas!
My Favorite Holiday
AMY CULLIFORD
CRABTREE
Publishing Company
www.crabtreebooks.com

School-to-Home Support for Caregivers and Teachers

This book helps children grow by letting them practice reading. Here are a few guiding questions to help the reader build his or her comprehension skills. Possible answers appear here in red.

Before Reading:

- What do I think this book is about?
  - *I think this book is about Christmas.*
  - *I think this book is about how children celebrate Christmas.*
- What do I want to learn about this topic?
  - *I want to learn more about how Christmas is celebrated in different countries.*
  - *I want to learn why we give presents on Christmas.*

During Reading:

- I wonder why...
  - *I wonder why many people put up a Christmas tree.*
  - *I wonder why Santa brings gifts on Christmas.*
- What have I learned so far?
  - *I have learned that red and green are Christmas colors.*
  - *I have learned that carolers are people who sing Christmas carols.*

After Reading:

- What details did I learn about this topic?
  - *I have learned that Santa brings gifts on Christmas.*
  - *I have learned that some people like to sing Christmas carols.*
- Read the book again and look for the vocabulary words.
  - *I see the word **Christmas** on page 3 and the word **gift** on page 11. The other vocabulary words are found on page 14.*

It is **Christmas** Day!

We put up a
Christmas tree.

I see three **carolers.**

I see red and green all around.

I open a big **gift**.

It is from **Santa**!

Word List

Sight Words

a	day	it	three
and	from	open	up
all	green	put	we
around	I	red	
big	is	see	

Words to Know

carolers

Christmas

Christmas tree

gift

Santa

30 Words

It is **Christmas** Day!

We put up a **Christmas tree**.

I see three **carolers.**

I see red and green all around.

I open a big **gift**.

It is from **Santa**!

My Favorite Holiday

Written by: Amy Culliford

Designed by: Bobbie Houser

Series Development: James Earley

Proofreader: Petrice Custance

Educational Consultant: Marie Lemke M.Ed.

Photographs:

t = Top, c = Center, b = Bottom, l = Left, r = Right

Shutterstock: Sandra Cunningham: cover, p. 3, 14; Yuganov Konstantin: p. 1; Monstar Studio: p. 5, 14; Marcos Castillo: p. 7, 14; Jenn Huls: p. 8 tl; AGCuesta: p. 8 tr; Roman Samborskyi: p. 8 bl; Elena Shashkina: p. 8 br; JeniFoto: p. 9 t; magicoven: p. 9 bl; New Africa: p. 9 br; Lucky Business: p. 10, 14; Kiselev Andrey Valerevich: p. 13-14

Library and Archives Canada Cataloguing in Publication

CIP available at Library and Archives Canada

Library of Congress Cataloging-in-Publication Data

CIP available at Library of Congress

Crabtree Publishing Company

www.crabtreebooks.com 1-800-387-7650

Printed in the USA/072022/CG20220201

 In Canada: We acknowledge the financial support of the Government of Canada through the Canada Book Fund for our publishing activities.

Published in the United States
Crabtree Publishing
347 Fifth Avenue, Suite 1402-145
New York, NY, 10016

Published in Canada
Crabtree Publishing
616 Welland Ave.
St. Catharines, ON, L2M 5V6